REN MILLARD

GET THE TRUTH

The Ultimate Guide to Objective and Subjective Truth, Discover The Difference Between Subjective and Objective Truth and When to Use Them

Descrierea CIP a Bibliotecii Naționale a României
REN MILLARD
GET THE TRUTH. The Ultimate Guide to Objective and Subjective Truth, Discover The Difference Between Subjective and Objective Truth and When to Use Them / Ren Millard – Bucharest: Editura My Ebook, 2020
ISBN

REN MILLARD

GET THE TRUTH
The Ultimate Guide to Objective and Subjective Truth, Discover The Difference Between Subjective and Objective Truth and When to Use Them

My Ebook Publishing House
Bucharest, 2020

TABLE OF CONTENTS

Chapter 1: Subjective Thinking Basics 7

Chapter 2: Objective Thinking Basics 9

Chapter 3: When to Be Objective 11

Chapter 4: When to Be Subjective 13

Chapter 5: Easy Ways to Remember Objective 17

Chapter 6: Easy Ways to Remember Subjective 19

Chapter 7: Examples of Objective Thinking 22

Chapter 8: Examples of Subjective Thinking 26

Chapter 9: What Happens When You Don't Have A Clear Vision 29

Chapter 10: Benefits of Objective Thinking 33

Chapter 11: Benefits of Subjective Thinking 39

FOREWORD

In newspapers, stories or spoken words, many people across the world are confused between subjective and objective thinking. Some think objectively, but the truth is, they're really thinking subjectively.

For this reason, many are confused with the truth as they don't have any idea on what they really think. More often than not, some try to bombarding with facts as well as figures.

It depends on you to create order within your thinking patterns, which will help you understand the truth and the false. In order for you to do this, knowing the difference between objective and subjective thinking is a wise decision. In this book, one will gain knowledge about subjective thinking and objective thinking as well.

CHAPTER 1

SUBJECTIVE THINKING BASICS

Synopsis

Many people have various misconceptions between subjective thinking and objective thinking for the reason that they don't the difference of these two. As a result, most of them end up confused and fail to know what subjective thinking is all about.

Subjective Thinking Defined

Subjective thinking has a huge difference from objective thinking. It is because this revolves on the statement that has been colored by people. This is often based on reality, yet it reflects the perspective by with how the speaker views reality.

This can't be verified with the use of concrete facts as well as figures.

More often than not, subjective thinking revolves around your experiences, opinions or discussions of an object. Many people don't know that they are thinking subjectively due to the reason that when they have a particular object, they think that they are being objective. That is a misconception. It is because subjective thinking only becomes objective when you are just using an object without relating yourself into it. Keep in mind that subjective is when there's nothing tangible in the situation.

Subjective thinking plays a huge role when making decisions. According to experts, your impression or opinion for something let you think efficiently. This just means that you are thinking subjectively as you are relating some experiences in your life. Plus, you are not using a particular object when thinking.

With those basics in mind, knowing the difference between subjective and objective is now much easier. Therefore, if you want to know how different subjective and objective is, always keep in mind those mentioned details above as this can make a difference and can offer you clear vision when knowing the truth and finding out the difference.

CHAPTER 2

OBJECTIVE THINKING BASICS

Synopsis

Objective thinking revolves around having thoughts that are unbiased. It's not touched by the experiences or tastes of the person or speaker. It's verifiable through looking up facts or doing mathematical calculations.

What You Need to Know about Objective Thinking

As its name implies, objective thinking involves object. If you are in a store full of products, you are thinking objectively when you are trying to choose the finest one. But, once you have involved your opinions in the situation, you are being subjective.

Not all people know about subjective and objective thinking. Some just think and think for an answer or anything until they have arrived on a wrong decision. Due to this, many people end up miserable because of making wrong decisions. If you don't want this to happen to you, thinking objectively is a good idea.

Objective thinking only happens when you are dealing with objects. There are various cases that you are objective. One is when you are purchasing items like what mentioned above. Another is when you are in an art gallery searching for a masterpiece that would suit your home décor or room theme.

When you are making figures for your calculations, you are also being objective. There are a lot of things that you are objective. But, despite from knowing its difference from subjective, objective thinking may also give you tons of benefits. Both subjective and objective thinking can offer you benefits. So, if you want to reap wonderful benefits, start by thinking objective as this will let you stay on the right track.

CHAPTER 3
WHEN TO BE OBJECTIVE

Synopsis

Not all knows when to be objective. That is why many encounter some issues especially when it comes to thinking subjectively. If you are one of those who are experiencing difficulties on when to be objective, this chapter will give you a glimpse of how and when you will be objective.

When Is the Right Time to Be Objective?

It is essential to be objective whenever you are creating any sort of a rational decision. This might involve buying something or deciding that offer to take. There are other instances on when you should objective and that includes the following:

Reading Books When Shopping Around

Some people think that when they are reading. They are thinking subjectively. But, what they don't know is that they thinking objectively especially when they are reading some details about deals or job offers. Another example of thinking objectively is when you are reading newspapers and other sources about news.

There are also instances that some may think subjectively when reading most particularly if the reader relates some of the parts on the story.

Meeting or Having Discussions

Meeting or having discussions with some people is also objective thinking. This provides anyone the ability to concentrate or focus on their goals rather than being emotional during the meeting. Therefore, if you want your co-employees or employees to focus or take your words seriously, always remember to be objective as this will help you become a better employee or a role model in your workplace. You have to take note that meetings or discussions are a serious thing. So, always choose to be objective as this will offer you more benefits in the long run.

Purchasing Items

Whenever you are purchasing beauty products, gadgets or whatever items that you need, you should think objectively when purchasing some products. The reason behind it is that these items are not something that you can connect your experiences or some things in your life. They are objects and you need to be specific with your needs in order for you to get the finest items that would match to your needs or preferences.

Solving Equations

When you are solving equations, you have to keep in mind that you are thinking objectively. The reason behind it is that you are describing something like an object. But, there are also cases when solving equations become subjective. It is when the problem involves persons or any characters. That is the reason why there's a difference.

Holding a Piece of Art

Any piece of art is an object. Whether you are planning to buy a piece of art or you are just holding a piece of art, you are being objective. However, if you want to be subjective, you should discuss the art you see. Your opinions are subjective. Although you are holding a piece of art, your opinions make a difference.

There are other things that you need for you to be objective. So, when dealing with those scenarios above, always remember to be objective. This will let you decide efficiently without requiring you to be confused or made some wrong decisions, which may just because you inconvenience in the end.

CHAPTER 4

WHEN TO BE SUBJECTIVE

Synopsis

Some people know how to be subjective, but only few who knows when. If you are one of those who are confused with subjective and objective, you must learn both have their own differences. So, in this chapter, learn how and when to be objective.

When is the Right Time to be Subjective?

Subjective thinking can be used when nothing tangible is at the scenario. These following will you know on when to be subjective:

Watching Movie

You have to take note that being subjective involves experiences in one's life or relating something that is connected to your life and the persons around you. That is the reason why when you are watching movies, you should consider being subjective. It is because you are relating some scenes in your life. Another reason is that there are movies that may be familiar with your traits or past experiences. With this, it makes you experience fun and enjoyment.

Reading for Pleasure

Reading for pleasure is also like watching movies. More often than not, there are stories that you may relate with. Through this, you are being subjective. However, purchasing a book is a different story because you are being objective.

Discussing Any Sort of Art

If you always love to be in a particular art exhibit, discussing any sort of art is objective. Since you are pertaining to an object, you have to take note that you are not being subjective, but you are being objective because you are describing an art or an object in the art you see.

CHAPTER 5

EASY WAYS TO REMEMBER OBJECTIVE

Synopsis

If you are still confused between objective and subjective, there is nothing to worry about because there are simple ways to remember objective. With these, being objective will not be difficult for you. In addition to that, you will be able to distinguish objective thinking efficiently without the need to be confused or without requiring to ask for help from an expert.

Best Ways to Remember Objective

Objective thinking can be remembered easily compared to subjective thinking. The reason behind it is that objective sounds like the term object. Whenever you are dealing with an object, you are being objective especially when you are touching or holding it.

The things that will help you remind of being objective is by holding or involving concrete or solid objects. There are easy ways to remember being objective and these are:

- ***You are objective if you are dealing with concrete or solid objects.*** Whether you are planning to purchase or just shop around in your local store, you are being objective when you touch or hold things. However, if you are dealing in an online store, this may make a difference. It is because you are only objective if you are touching objects that you require for shopping. In online shopping, you don't have to touch objects as all items available are virtual. It will only become objective once you have received the items you purchased. Many said that shopping online can be subjective most particularly if you are reading feedbacks or reviews of the product.

- ***Eating in a restaurant.*** Eating in restaurants also involve thinking. You are being objective if you will start to eat. But, there will be times when you are going to be subjective. It is when you will have discussions with your companion. Your opinions with what you can be somewhat subjective. However, in most cases, it is objective because foods are also items.

- ***Playing sports.*** For those who are an addict in various sports, you are being objective because you are dealing with objects like balls. But, when you start a meeting with your co-players, you are being subjective. It is because this is the time that you will be able to analyze and make decisions successfully.

There are other simple ways to remember objective. But, the simplest way of remembering it is by keeping in mind objects. Whenever there are objects involved, expect that you are being objective with what you see and with what you think. So, remember those things above as they will give you the results you want especially if you are aiming something objectively.

Just remember to take note of their difference because this will let you know the real things behind the truth. This will also give you a vision and will allow you to stay on the right track no matter how tough everything is.

CHAPTER 6

EASY WAYS TO REMEMBER SUBJECTIVE

Synopsis

Subjective thinking is the opposite of objective thinking. You cannot point to subjective subjects. They are all kept in your head as well as your past experiences. Subjective opinions are not permanent and subject to various factors that may range from facts to emotions. If you are still confused with subjective, there are ways on how you can remember it.

What Are the Ways to Remember Subjective?

There are plenty of ways on how you can remember subjective. Whatever your profession is, these ways will help you think subjectively in an efficient manner. Some of these are:

Opinions

When you are making opinions or heard them, you have to keep in mind all the time that these are subjective. Subjective thinking involves your opinions on particular things. No matter how harsh they are, you are being subjective. Take note that you are only objective when you are touching things or objects that you see around you. But, once you have made opinions about them, you are thinking subjectively.

Past Experiences

Thinking or knowing your past experiences is subjective. It is because these do not involve objects or things. Your past experiences also involve various emotions. Your experiences may be sad or happy. But, no matter what the emotions involved, you are being subjective. Therefore, whenever you are thinking of your past experiences because of reading, watching a movie or telling your stories to other people, you are subjective. The subjects don't matter. As long as there are no objects involved, you are subjective.

Emotions

Emotions are also another way that you are being subjective. With these, you will easily figure out that you are thinking subjectively not objectively. Therefore, whenever you are dealing with emotions, whether you are at home or workplace, you are being subjective.

Feedbacks or Comments

When reading feedbacks or comments online or in newspapers, you are subjective. No matter what the subject is, you are subjective once you have read comments or feedbacks from any person. However, if you are going to feedback by relying on a particular object, you are being objective. So, be careful when you encounter this scenario. It is because this has a huge difference and may matter in the long run most particularly if you are going to make decisions out of your thoughts or feedbacks you have made.

Reactions on Something

Whether your reaction is violent or not, this is still another way to remember subjective. Since your reactions or comments also involve your feelings or emotions on a certain subject, this means that you are being subjective.

CHAPTER 7

EXAMPLES OF OBJECTIVE THINKING

Synopsis

Now that you know when to be objective and ways to remember objective, it is now the best time to find out the examples of objective thinking. There are several examples of objective thinking. Through these, one will be able to distinguish objective from subjective without the need to be confused with various thoughts they have in mind.

Examples of Objective Thinking

There are lots of examples of objective thinking. Some of them are but not limited to:

Scientific Facts

Scientific facts are objective because most of them are backed up with objects. For instance, when you are dealing with fossils, you are being objective because they will not tell you the things that happened from the past. You will rely their years of existence, uses or purposes on their physical appearance. Through several tests, you will know what they are made of and how they are made without depending on the opinions of other experts as they can't tell these facts.

Professions

There are several professions who are practicing objective thinking. One of these is the veterinarians. Since animals can't talk to vets about what they are feeling or what pain they are experiencing, vets rely on the physical attributes of the animals. They can't depend on what the facial expressions of the animals. They can't even conclude their diseases by seeing something on their body. But, in order for them to do this, they should consider several tests that will allow them to know the truth and the accurate things regarding their diseases or what they feel in their body. With these tests, they can assure that they are on the right track of knowing the diseases of the animals.

Another profession that is practicing objective thinking is law enforcement groups. They can't just say that the case is true or false by relying on their opinions or comments from other people who have seen the crime. Their judgment should rely on the objects that are involved in the scene. With these, they will be able to know the real and truth behind those that happened.

Observing the Weather

More often than not, many people believed with what other people say when it comes to weather. But, what they don't know is that observing the weather can be objective. The reason behind it is that weather can't tell them anything about the temperature or anything that would relate to it. Through observing the weather, one will know if it will be a sunny or rainy day.

There are other examples that will let you think objectively. But, those are the common examples that most people encounter. So, if you want to think objectively, make sure that you keep in mind those examples provided above because they can be your guide.

CHAPTER 8

EXAMPLES OF SUBJECTIVE THINKING

Synopsis

Subjective thinking isn't the same with objective thinking. You don't have to rely on objects just to make your thoughts. All you need is to hear or relate things on your experiences. But, there are other examples of subjective thinking. Through these, knowing subjective will not be tough for you.

Common Examples of Subjective Thinking

There are different examples of subjective thinking. If you are one those who want to differentiate between objective and subjective, these examples will keep you on the right track:

Interpretations

One of the most common examples of subjective thinking is interpretations. The reason why interpretations are subjective is because people rely on what they want to express on particular things. Although there are objects involved when interpreting, interpretations are still subjective as you will depend your interpretations on what you feel or experience with the things involved. There are also cases when the subject involved is subjective. That is the reason why interpretations are subjective.

Opinions

Opinions are also one of the examples of subjective thinking. This becomes subjective because people don't use objects to make opinions. When they are making opinions, they do it by connecting their past experiences with a particular subject. For example, if your friend is broken-hearted and ask for your opinion about what he or she planning to do, you will give your own opinion based from what you have learned or experienced from your past.

You don't just say something because you have read it from one of your books. You have said it as you already experienced it before. Through your experiences, you can give your opinions. This can be done without relying on objects around you, but with what you feel and experienced before.

Marketing Presentation or Any Kind of Presentation

In marketing presentation or any kind of presentation, you are also subjective. It is because you are discussing something that you see or presented in front of you. Although this may involve touching remote control or navigating your laptop, this is still subjective because you are already discussing the things on your presentation and you are using your mind to discuss. Therefore, whenever you are presenting something in front of many people, take note that you are subjective, not objective. It only becomes objective when you stop discussing and you start to use your laptop for games or anything for pleasure.

There are other examples of subjective thinking. With those mentioned above, you will easily know that you are subjective. The best thing about these examples is that you will not be confused between subjective and objective thinking. Once you have encountered those, you will easily determine that you are subjective.

CHAPTER 9

WHAT HAPPENS WHEN YOU DON'T HAVE A CLEAR VISION

Synopsis

One of the reasons why many people struggle to find out the truth and be a leader of their own selves is that they do not have a clear vision. Having a vision is essential as this can guide anyone on their path or journey. This will also help one to stay on the right track even if he or she is distracted by a mix of thoughts. But, what happens when you don't have a clear vision?

The Results of Having No Clear Vision

There are many things that may happen if you don't have clear vision. Some of these are:

- **Confusions**

If you don't have a clear vision, one of the things that may happen is that you will be confused with everything. You have to keep in mind that visions are the things that will let you stay on the right path. If you are confused, the tendency is you will always be distracted that comes on your way. Once these mixed up, you will not be able to know the truth and you might end up failing in achieving your goals. Whether you want to be successful in the future or you just want to know the truth, a clear vision plays a huge role.

- **Loss of Focus or Concentration**

Having no clear visions also means that there's a huge possibility that you will lose your focus or concentration. Since you are always confused, concentration may be a tough job for you as you will not be able to think subjectively or objectively. That is the reason why a clear vision is a must for you to get going.

- **You Will See No Progress**

Achieving success isn't something that can be done overnight. That is why you need to stick with your vision. But, if you don't have a vision, you might not see any progress. Due to this, it can be hard for you to take another step in your journey, which is not a good thing especially for those who have targeted goals when they reached a specific age.

There are other things that may happen if you will not have a clear vision. But, there's a way for you to make a clear vision. These following can be of great help:

- **Determine What You Want to Accomplish**

Instead of thinking about the benefits or perks of your goals in life, focus on conceiving purposes. What do you like to accomplish? What is vital for you? Why is it important? You have to be specific with your goals. If you can't memorize them, write them out for you to have a reminder.

- **Know Your Time Frame**

Knowing your time frame can help you complete your goals. When thinking about your time frame, you should be realistic. Don't consider a certain time frame if you can't reach it. Be general when you're reaching your goal.

- **Have a List of Your Actions**

Aside from knowing what you like to achieve, you should also know how to do it as this can be vital. When knowing your actions, think of the end results you like to create. Then, consider exactly what you really need for you to take little steps.

- **Have a Solid Plan**

If you want to have a clear vision, you should start with a solid plan for you to take action. This plan will let you surpass everything no matter how tough or simple the obstacles are. In addition, always make sure that you will put your plans into actions.

With those ways above, having a clear vision will never be your issue as you will be able to achieve what you desire. Moreover, this will lead you to a fast track to success.

Benefits of Having a Clear Vision

Once you have a clear vision in your life, there are tons of benefits you can enjoy. You will be able to experience the following:

- **No Confusions**

If you have a clear vision, you will not be confused with your thoughts or what you want to do in your life. Regardless of what you want to aim in life, your vision will fuel you up, which will enable you to get your desired results in no time. Having no confusions can also keep you strong on your journey. With this, you will be able to surpass anything that you may face no matter how tough it is.

- **Achieve Success in No Time**

Achieving success is really a tough job. There are various obstacles that may encounter and there are also things that may weaken you. That is the reason why vision plays an important role for you to get going. So, always have a vision for you to achieve success in no time.

- **Stay on the Right Track**

The best thing about having a vision is that you will not be confused with what you aim. This just means that you will be able to stay on the right track even though things are a bit tricky and tough.

With the mentioned benefits of having a clear vision, there are no reasons why you should not have one. So, if you don't want to experience the results of having no vision, consider the ways on how you can make a clear vision without the need to be confused.

CHAPTER 10

BENEFITS OF OBJECTIVE THINKING

Synopsis

Although determining objective thinking is not easy, there are benefits you can enjoy. With these, you will have the chance to grab the opportunity of objective thinking by knowing how to make the most of it and how you can perform it easily.

Some Benefits of Objective Thinking

There are various perks you can enjoy once you have used objective thinking wisely. These benefits are as follows:

No Wrongful Judgments

Unlike subjective thinking, you will not make wrongful judgments. It is because the facts will be based on the objects not on what other people said to you. With this, you will be able to avoid judgments, which cause some problems in the future. Also, this will let you avoid hurting some people because of your judgments.

Being Able to Know the Truth Based on the Given Objects

Like vets, there are instances that you don't need to let anyone tell you what they feel or experiencing. Using the objects or through the physical characteristics of a person, you will know the truth even without being confused with the thoughts you have made through listening to what people say.

Another example is the law enforcement professionals who also based their conclusion on the objects they have seen. With these, they will be able to know the truth as the objects show the real thing regarding the truth.

There are other benefits you can enjoy from objective thinking. Those are just few. So, start reaping those benefits now and find out what it can do for your life.

CHAPTER 11

BENEFITS OF SUBJECTIVE THINKING

Synopsis

Subjective thinking was already practiced by many people. Even professionals are practicing these because they can get benefits from this kind of finding out the truth. Whatever your profession is, whether you are a teacher or a computer engineer, there are many benefits you can enjoy.

These benefits will give you the reason why you should practice it sometimes. Subjective thinking was already practiced by everyone centuries ago. Ever since people were born, they are already capable of being subjective because the world comprises every subject that will let anyone interpret, make opinions, and present what they want.

The Perks of Being a Subjective Thinker

Now that you already have knowledge about subjective thinking, it is time to know the perks that you can get from subjective thinking. These are as follows:

Improve Your Skills in Analyzing Things

The best thing about subjective thinking is that you will be able to improve your skills in analyzing things. Since you will be using your mind every time without the need to use objects as your basis, you will be able to improve your skills in analyzing things. With this, it will be much easier for you to analyze everything.

Boost Your Knowledge

Subjective thinking can also boost your knowledge. Through brainstorming, you will be able to know the things that you don't have a clue with the help of discussions with your friends and other people that surround you. So, being a person who always utilizes subjective thinking can offer you the knowledge that may be beneficial in the long run.

Being Able to Make Interpretations Efficiently

Interpretations are important to everyone especially for those who have professions that require interpretations to accomplish their work. That is the reason why interpretations can be efficient to anyone as this will allow them to create interpretations in a successful manner.

Make Decisions Successfully

Making decisions is not easy. That is the reason why you subjective thinking plays a huge role. Through this, you can make decisions successfully without experiencing any difficulty.

There are other benefits you can reap from subjective thinking. Just see to it that you are using it wisely in order for you to experience the most of their benefits.

www.ingramcontent.com/pod-product-compliance
Ingram Content Group UK Ltd.
Pitfield, Milton Keynes, MK11 3LW, UK
UKHW022213230426
12048UKWH00016BA/820